EIR (ISSN 0273-6314) *is published weekly (50 issues), by EIR News Service, Inc., P.O. Box 17390, Washington, D.C. 20041-0390. (703) 777-9451*

European Headquarters: E.I.R. GmbH, Postfach Bahnstrasse 9a, D-65205, Wiesbaden, Germany
Tel: 49-611-73650
Homepage: http://www.eirna.com
e-mail: eirna@eirna.com
Director: Georg Neudecker

Montreal, Canada: 514-461-1557

Denmark: EIR - Danmark, Sankt Knuds Vej 11, basement left, DK-1903 Frederiksberg, Denmark. Tel.: +45 35 43 60 40, Fax: +45 35 43 87 57. e-mail: eirdk@hotmail.com.

Mexico City: EIR, Sor Juana Inés de la Cruz 242-2 Col. Agricultura C.P. 11360 Delegación M. Hidalgo, México D.F. Tel. (5525) 5318-2301 eirmexico@gmail.com

Obama Organized An Act of War

LaRouche: Obama Organized An Act of War

Nov. 24—Lyndon LaRouche today responded to the Turkish shoot-down of a Russian fighter plane by declaring that "Obama organized an act of war, and has thus endangered the United States, as well as all of humanity."

Qualified American figures have emphasized, in the immediate wake of the Turkish actions, that Turkey's President Erdogan would never have taken this action if he did not know, in advance, that he had tacit support from Obama. Those sources observed that Obama was furious over the weekend that the French government, under tremendous popular pressure, was moving towards a real alliance with Russia to destroy ISIS. In stark contrast to that sane French response to the Paris attacks of Nov. 13, Obama has renewed his demands that the ouster of Syrian President Bashar Assad must happen immediately, and must precede the actions against the Islamic State.

LaRouche called for Obama's immediate removal from office. "Obama's actions constitute a potential act of war, and he must be kicked out of office. Otherwise, making any further excuses for Obama, in light of the events of today, poses a threat to all of the world, because it could lead to general war." LaRouche added that "the prospect of impeachment is hanging in the air."

Humiliate Him! Denounce Anyone That Won't!

Nov 25—A few hours after releasing the statement above, LaRouche told a meeting of associates that it was not adequate; he had more to say on the subject.

He said that anyone who supports or tolerates Obama in the Presidency is a traitor, unfit for human company. We must draw the line here! He is beyond redemption,—evil,—a Satanic force. Don't pretend you can find some other interpretation. We are on the edge of thermonuclear war; our only hope is that a limited number of people can intervene from the inside against Obama. We must denounce anyone who won't denounce him.

"Don't imagine that I'm exaggerating," LaRouche said. "I'm not and I don't. We must shun and denounce anyone who won't denounce Obama as evil."

The fate of humanity now depends upon that. We must break Obama's morale,—intimidate him. He must see the people immediately around him humiliating him in his presence. "Oh! President Shithead!" Why shithead? "You don't have any brains!"

Don't try to find some other explanation; This is real. If you don't do this now, there is no other refuge for you.

We must demoralize him! Do it now, not in a couple of weeks. Each of you must learn that; that's the message. There is no other way: it doesn't exist,—only the immediate threat of thermonuclear war.

The time has come to humiliate the bastard; and if you find cowards who know better but won't do that, humiliate *them* as cowards. This is a matter of warfare, not of opinion; It's one of those times where you don't fool around. "Shut him down, or you're all dead. I haven't said this recently, but I'm saying it tonight." Focus on the Manhattan area, and go further. Europe won't do it; China and Russia, by themselves, are not enough to do it alone. You have to do it.

Destroy his ego: that's what we must do. No other option exists. Are you afraid of him? Look at the number of people he has killed!

This defines the future of our organization from this point on.

Overthrow the British Monarchy!

Nov. 22—With Brussels in a second day of lockdown in anticipation of another major Islamic State terrorist attack on the scale of the Nov. 13 massacres in Paris, attention is increasingly turning to the fact that the hub of jihadist terrorism is actually located in the heart of Europe. Brussels, the capital of both NATO and the European Union, is now being referred to as Brusselstan, just as London has long been referred to as Londonistan, because virtually every jihadist, narco, and separatist terrorist organization has been housed, protected, and financed by the British Monarchy. Recently, the British government dropped all charges against an alleged jihadist weapons smuggler, because his defense attorneys pointed out that the same groups he was accused of arming were being overtly backed by British intelligence's MI6.

This is an old story. London has been at the center of world terrorism for decades. In January 2000 *Executive Intelligence Review* provided a dossier to the U.S. Department of State in 2000, calling for Great Britain to be put on the list of state sponsors of terrorism. The dossier was based exclusively on evidence provided by governments around the world, including Russia, Egypt, India, Pakistan, Colombia, and Peru; it showed conclusively that the British Crown was harboring the world's worst terrorists as part of the system of Empire. The biggest British banks, starting with HSBC (formerly the Hong Kong and Shanghai Banking Corporation, of Opium Wars infamy), are the world's most notorious drug money laundering institutions, as recently documented by the United States Senate.

It is the British Crown, as well, that has deployed Knight Commander John Schellnhuber to capture the Pope and the Vatican for the idea of radical population reduction, based on the scientific swindle of man-induced global warming.

Every atrocity committed by President Barack Obama—from his drone-kill mass assassinations in Afghanistan, Pakistan, Yemen, and Somalia, to his overthrow and cold-blooded murder of Qadaffi in Libya, creating a zone of chaos, terrorism, and failed states across much of North Africa and the Middle East, to the decimation of the conditions of life for the vast majority of Americans—can be laid at the doorstep of the British Crown. Obama is nothing but a British agent, who was selected by the British to be installed as President of the United States, on behalf of the Crown and the City of London.

After the Paris atrocities, it is becoming transparently obvious to a growing number of thinking people that the Islamic State is a creation of Obama and the British. Al-Qaeda was created and nurtured by the British, the United States, and Saudi Arabia during the 1980s, who collectively assembled a gang of terrorists from jails throughout the Arab and Islamic world to drive the Soviets out of Afghanistan. In 1985, Prince Bandar bin Sultan, a virtual member of the Bush Family, joined with British Prime Minister Margaret Thatcher to launch the al-Yamamah barter arrangement, under which a $100 billion offshore slush fund was established to covertly arm al-Qaeda and other terrorist outfits. In 2001, Bandar deployed some of those al-Yamamah funds to bankroll the 9/11 hijackers to take down the World Trade Towers and strike the Pentagon.

If you want to understand why British agent Barack Obama has refused to declassify the 28 pages from the original Joint Congressional Inquiry into 9/11, you must start from the top down, with this account of how the British and Obama created al-Qaeda and, more recently, the Islamic State. Former Defense Intelligence Agency head Gen. Michael Flynn has openly reported that President Obama armed the Syrian rebels out of Benghazi, and continued to do so because it was the Administration's policy. DIA documents from the Summer and Autumn of 2012 detailed the joint British-American operations from Benghazi to smuggling ports in rebel-held areas of Syria.

Lyndon LaRouche bluntly told colleagues on Sunday, Nov. 22, that you have to eradicate the British Monarchy or there is no solution to the Syria war or any other global hot-spot. Unless the British Empire is brought down, we are facing global war against Russia and China, leading to the extermination of much of mankind. Barack Obama is a British agent, selected by the British to be President of the United States. We must sink the British Empire and all it represents, or we will face accelerated horror shows around the globe.

EIR Contents

www.larouchepub.com Volume 42, Number 47, November 27, 2015

Cover This Week

Russian TV1 depiction of the flight pattern of the Russian jet downed by the Turks. Shown 12:13 AM Moscow Time, Nov. 25.

Man's Destiny in the Universe

Part of a discussion of Lyndon LaRouche with associates on Nov. 21, 2015

LaRouche: The point is, we're dealing with a global situation. We're so restricted by the way we even think about a global situation, because we live in a city, and an area, and a larger area. Most people in the United States and Europe are idiots when it comes to actual assessment of what the implications are.

Haven't we by now learned from Kepler and beyond on the Galactic System, that there is no such thing as an Earth system? The Earth system is an aspect of a larger system. We haven't learned that because we're still memorizing gibberish of the type that we get in the United States and elsewhere; it's gibberish.

Where's the future of mankind located? And if it's not the future of mankind, why are you bothering about it? The question is, what are the issues of the existence of mankind as a species? Now, as far as we know now, Ben [Deniston] will come out some time with some water from the Galactic System; but that's not the limit to the thing. It's a multiple Galactic System, and there are things beyond it—effects beyond that.

And mankind has to realize that those processes, combined with the significance of the human mind—the human mind is the only thing that's important. And it's how you treat the human mind and how you use it which defines the destiny of mankind. All these little fantasies about this part of history, that part of history, are all fantasies; because mankind has to operate on a basis which is galactic. Otherwise mankind has no clear purpose.

You Have to Go to a Higher Level

And people talk about people who are dead —"Oh, they died." Well, what do you mean they died? You mean they're not significant? Many of them are not significant in terms of their behavior. But this kind of thing—the popular opinion—I *despise* popular opinion; I see nothing but evil in popular opinion. Or it's ignorance, which is about the same thing.

So, that's what we have to do. We have to realize what we're dealing with; mankind has reached a point where mankind can no longer play tiddlywinks with history. We are part of beyond the Solar System entirely; we're in the Galactic System and beyond that. That's where our destiny is located. And our destiny is located in the future of mankind; in the optimal level of mankind.

NASA/JPL-Caltech

Beyond our Solar System: This artist's concept shows the Voyager 1 spacecraft entering interstellar space, which is dominated by plasma, ionized gas (illustrated here as a brownish haze) which was thrown off by giant stars millions of years ago.

When you think in those terms, then you begin to think. Otherwise, you're just like a dummy; you're going through the motions like a dummy on the stage. And we have to operate on a truly global basis; otherwise, we don't know what the future is. If we define everything in this restricted area, you don't know what the future is; you're just talking. You're babbling, reciting words that don't mean anything. And now we realize that mankind's future depends upon things that most governments refuse to acknowledge as existing.

And we're all practical; everyone's practical. And practical people are idiots, if they even aspire to that high level of achievement. You want to collect bones? Be a dog.

No, we've got to cut this stuff out about all these interpretations of things; it's nonsense. There's no reality to it. When you look at the Galactic System and realize that the Galactic System exists, and there's a highly complicated process which you cannot overlook; you cannot just predetermine that. By now we should know that you don't have that kind of knowledge of the actual power to adduce things in that way. You have to go to a higher level which has always been mankind's destiny; to go to a higher level than mankind had ever imagined.

And it's by doing that, that mankind is able to progress and find the meaning of the existence of mankind. And only then are you really a person who understands humanity. Until you know what the future of mankind is, as mankind has never known it fully beforehand, that's when you get the ability to judge what the future holds.

Jeff Steinberg: There've been some NASA discussions with the Russians and with the Chinese in the past week; and the basic message is that the next phase of work in space requires collaboration among the top scientists of a number of major nations for it to be successful. So it's an area where what you've been saying about the old concept of nation-state, has to be superseded by defining certain key missions that are in the common interests of mankind as a whole.

NASA

Five NASA astronauts and a Russian cosmonaut, pictured in the tunnel between the Space Shuttle Discovery and the SPACEHAB module in 2011.

LaRouche: The idea of the nation-state is actually something which holds mankind down and backward; because by now all the evidence we have in terms of science, is that we have not even begun to scratch the meaning of mankind, what mankind's function is. And it's what we can create from the development of the future that counts. People get so tied up with involvement in what they think their personal destiny is; and that's too small a way to speak of mankind.

Ben Deniston: When you talk about science and the Galaxy, the problem is that people still think of it as an objective thing. You're just figuring out what this stuff out there is, and you're finding new discoveries of this stuff out there. But each day, you are transforming what the human species is.

LaRouche: Exactly.

The Meaning of Human Life
Deniston: You look at what Kepler did in the beginning, of moving mankind into really the level of the Solar System. Mentally, creatively, that created the basis for the human species to be a completely different species really. So there's no difference between these two; not technology, not innovation, but you're talking about the truly fundamental scientific discoveries.

LaRouche: Well, Kepler defined that. Kepler took the question of the mystery of what the Solar System means, and said that there's a law, there's a principle involved here. And it's a principle which is only awesome, an awesome experience; and when you see that awesome experience, you have the insight into something about mankind which you had never had access to before.

And you just take what Kepler did, the way he defined the question. That changes everything about what our knowledge of what mankind is; because you have the whole system, and the system is a system which does not conform to any system which had been known by man before. And the discovery by Kepler in terms of the modality of the function of the process of the Galactic System and so forth. The Galactic System is an extension of this.

Xinhua/CCTV

One of the many photos of the Moon's surface by the descending Chinese lunar probe Chang'e-3 on December 14, 2013.

Now, we're going into the Galactic System in a big way, relative to what we've known before. And that means we have to change what we think about mankind, to correspond to what we discover as being the powers of mankind which mankind has not discovered beforehand. When you want to say, "What's the meaning of my life?"—that's the question that defines the answer. And it's the devotion to the future of mankind, and the future development of mankind on a higher level than before, which defines the significance of mankind. All these practical things, "Oh, I came in with this story," and "I came in with the explanation,"—it's all crap. Long past crap.

The Dark Side of the Moon

No, our job is to create the future; and if you want to create the future, you have to be devoted to the actuality of the future.

And that's my big frustration; people don't understand the future. You see, mankind has to grow up; they all think that they inhabit a piece of flesh which is sooner or later going to disappear. And they don't understand what the meaning of human life is; and the meaning of human life is not located in one's own bones.

The meaning of human life is the advancement of mankind's ability to master the challenge of discovering the future of the universe. Nobody has ever discovered the universe; they haven't found it yet. They'll have to find it some time, I suppose, but they haven't done very well so far. They have merely the shadow of something of which they have no knowledge. And people should learn to be a bit more modest about these kinds of issues; to recognize the richness of their ignorance.

Steinberg: You look at specific things like the massive effort to prevent the breakthrough on fusion, because of what that represents in being able to do the kind of exploration of the Galaxy that opens up doors.

LaRouche: Well, you see that they're doing it in China, but they're not doing it in other parts of the world. And China, they're going behind the back side of the Moon, and the question of that which mankind does not otherwise actually see. And they're all so innocent that they just don't believe in the back side of the Moon; or they only have fantasies about it.

Some people in China have begun to get something beyond simple fantasies on this subject. And that's where China is making progress, while in the United States there are sits and farts. So, our job is to create the future; and you have to know what the future is in order to create it. And without that kind of orientation, you don't have the strength or intelligence to know how to deal with the future.

A Truly Human Identity Takes the Stage in *Silent Sky*

by Ian Overton and Kesha Rogers

Nov. 22—Prior to 1912, nobody could prove that the Milky Way was not the entire Universe. Henrietta Swan Leavitt's contribution to astrophysics changed that, although as a woman at Harvard, she was not even allowed to look through a telescope.

A powerful presentation of Henrietta Leavitt's life—and her passionate commitment to a creative intellectual identity—has been brought to the stage in Lauren Gunderson's play, *Silent Sky*. While little is actually known about the real Miss Leavitt—historians lack much correspondence and have no diaries—one can surmise enough to present, as Gunderson has, what must have been driving her to pursue the life she lived, facing the obstacles she faced.

This production, by Main Street Theater in Houston, Texas, directly counters the decades-long slump into populist *Regietheater* performances in which the director severely changes the original setting to shock or amuse the audience—and expresses clearly the profound quality that Friedrich Schiller taught in his essay, *Theater as a Moral Institution:*

> The theater is the common channel through which the light of wisdom streams down from the thoughtful, better part of society, spreading thence in mild beams throughout the entire state. More correct notions, more refined precepts, purer emotions flow from here into the veins of the people; the clouds of barbarism and gloomy superstition disperse; night yields to triumphant light.

The heroine of Silent Sky, *Henrietta Swan Leavitt, 1868-1921. Her discovery led to major changes in our understanding of the Universe.*

Determined Women Master the Stars' Destiny

In the play, Leavitt pursues her hypothesis about stars that go through a cycle of variation in brightness. She establishes that the length of the cycle is related to the star's intrinsic brightness (see box, next page). This discovery paved the way, shortly after her death in 1921, for Edwin Hubble and others to measure the distances of stars beyond the reach of visual parallax, which resulted in establishing that they were outside the Milky Way Galaxy. Leavitt's conclusion overturned existing theories about the limits of the universe. No, the Sun was not the center of the Galaxy. And the Galaxy was not the Universe or the center of the Universe.

Leavitt initially got no credit for her discovery as being a critical breakthrough leading to this result. After her death, however, Hubble said that she had deserved a Nobel Prize. The Swedish mathematician Gösta Mittag-Leffler recommended her for the prize, not knowing that she had died. It is never awarded posthumously.

The dozen or so women working at Harvard under Dr. Edward Pickering were not merely human "computers" (as they were called), but a cadre of scientific minds who classified tens of thousands of stars. In addition to Leavitt, two of the other women are included in the play, Annie Jump Cannon and Williamina Fleming, women who made well-known contributions in the field of astronomy and astrophysics. Throughout the play these women express agapic qualities of tough yet compassionate love, a collaborative sense of mission and discovery, and a mutual mentoring relationship with Henrietta, encouraging her in her passion for achieving her breakthrough. Henrietta too, pushed these women to be great.

Williamina Fleming ascended from her job as Pickering's housekeeper to the head of the computing group.

She became recognized in the astronomical community at large, examined the thermal spectra of more than 10,000 stars, and developed a classification system of 22 star classes according to the amount of hydrogen seen in their spectra.

Annie Jump Cannon is known as the theorist of stellar spectra. The major classes of stars were (and still are) known by a single letter in the sequence OBAF-GKM. Cannon coined the mnemonic phrase for this se-

NASA, ESA, and Hubble Heritage Team

Cepheid variable V1 in the Andromeda Galaxy.

How Far Is a Star?

Astronomers can only measure the distance to a star indirectly. For nearby stars, parallax can be used by viewing the star from two different points in the Earth's rotation. But Henrietta Leavitt made a discovery leading to the first indirect method for those stars too distant for parallax to work. She studied Cepheid variable stars and identified thousands of them, earning her a reputation as a "star finding fiend" among Harvard professors. Cepheids are a class of variable stars that vary in brightness (technically speaking, luminosity) because they expand and contract, which they do in regular, clock-like periods.

Leavitt discovered that brighter (hotter) Cepheids have longer periods, and dimmer (cooler) ones have shorter periods. Of course, a bright, distant star and a faint, nearby star can look equally bright to us; hence the distinction between intrinsic and apparent brightness. Leavitt compared Cepheids that were in one or the other of the two Magellanic Clouds—coherent bodies whose members have to all be at about the same distance from Earth (they are now known to

be two small, irregular galaxies close to our Galaxy). This meant that differences in brightness resulting from differences in distance were negligible, and this enabled her to discover the period-luminosity relationship: It was possible to identify the intrinsic luminosity of any Cepheid by measuring its period.

From her discovery, other astronomers realized that the distance of a galaxy can be determined by measuring the periods of its Cepheids, and then comparing the calculated intrinsic luminosity with the apparent luminosity. Hubble did this in 1923 with the star V1 in the spiral nebula that became known as the Andromeda Galaxy (or M31), proving that it was too far away to be part of our Galaxy.

Professor Pickering's "computers" at the Harvard College Observatory, pictured in 1890.

is. Throughout the play, the passionate character of Miss Leavitt moves the audience to understand that the true nature of human beings lies in the discovery of the unknown; we come to know the universe not through mathematical calculations, but through addressing paradoxes only recognizable and understood by the human mind.

This process is captured eloquently in the second act when Henrietta is weakened by cancer and questions the value of her contribution in the face of her own mortality and obscurity. Henrietta's devout sister Margaret challenges her on how their seemingly incompatible notions of God and science, heaven and the lasting effect of one's discovery of creation's laws on the world, are actually the same.

quence, still used today, "Oh, Be A Fine Girl—Kiss Me!" Later in life, as represented in the play, Cannon also became active in the Women's Suffrage movement of the 1920s.

Music of the Soul

Although Leavitt's two siblings died early in life, playwright Gunderson revives her sister, giving the two characters a profound relationship. In *Silent Sky,* Leavitt's hypothesis comes during a period of immense creative tension. She is represented at home listening to her sister play the piano, while her father is dying from the effects of a stroke; she is away from her laboratory and unsure of her suitor's faithfulness. Hearing the arpeggios, she connects the periodicity between the low and high notes, and the low and high luminosity of the variable stars, exclaiming, "I grasp it now! It's music! It's music!"

Wittingly or not, here Gunderson is reflecting what Lyndon LaRouche has emphasized as the very essence of the fight over the epistemology of science in the early Twentieth Century, as a battle between the soulless logical positivism of Bertrand Russell, and the immortal legacy of the creative individual dedicated to pursuing a discovery, even though she doesn't yet know what it

Like her contemporary Max Planck, Henrietta Leavitt gave up her original career choice as a concert pianist for physical science. Having lost most of her hearing, she picked up astronomy at the tail-end of her education at Radcliffe College, and went on to work at Harvard—for several years as an unpaid intern, and then for about 30 cents an hour (about $7.21 in 2015 wages).

What actually provoked Leavitt's hypothesis and discovery is not known, but such a musical representation is consistent with the same universal quality of genius found in such brilliant minds as Max Planck and Albert Einstein, who leaned heavily on their musical backgrounds to assist them when coming up against seeming limits to their creativity in their attempts to comprehend primary causes.

The Main Thing is the Effect

The founding artistic director of Houston's Main Street Theater, and director of *Silent Sky,* Rebecca Greene Udden, along with the other actor and actresses of the play, must have foreseen the profound effect this play would have on their audiences. They organized a series of talks following their performances of *Silent Sky* so that representatives of space science in the community could provide outlets for inspired attendees.

The speakers included Dr. Carolyn Summers, head of the astronomy section of the Houston Museum of Natural Sciences; Dr. Thomas Williams, professor emeritus at Rice University; Dr. Bonnie Dunbar, astronaut and former International Space Station (ISS) Commander; and Dr. Leroy Chiao, former ISS Commander, the first Chinese-American astronaut, and CEO of OneOrbit.

Representatives of the LaRouche movement attended these performances and discussions, and contributed to the already elevated discussion, raising the key epistemological elements of the play mentioned here, and inspiring the speakers to go beyond their existing conceptions.

Summers and Dunbar deplored the fact that today very few people even look at the sky to be inspired by it. For Bonnie Dunbar, as a child growing up in west Texas, "...observing the plane of our galaxy was a [nightly] fact of life." Now a professor at the University of Houston, she polemicized that only two or three of her 187 students even know there is an International Space Station; yet upwards of 80% of them erroneously believe that carbon dioxide is a pollutant. She pointed out that field trips to the local George Observatory inspire her students to become excited about discoveries that change their concepts about our potential future.

LaRouche PAC organizer Joseph Jennings raised the problem of Bertrand Russell's *Principia Mathematica* in this context, pointing out that the subordination of scientific passion to pre-ordained mathematical rules has eliminated discovery from among the joys of human life, to which Williams exclaimed, "I agree with you! We've stopped looking for causality—that's a problem."

Chiao said that the play and the achievements of Henrietta Leavitt inspired him to include the arts as part of OneOrbit's focus on bringing science, technology, engineering, and mathematics into school programs. LaRouche PAC Policy Committee member Kesha Rogers posed to Chiao that *Silent Sky* reminds us that space is not about mere profits nor the planting of flags out somewhere on the cheap, but about discovery and the profound sense of wonder about the vastness of

Leavitt: "I grasp it now! It's music! It's music!"

Universe that the human mind can know and love, as was demonstrated through the life of Henrietta Leavitt. She asked for his thoughts on how plays like this could revive a national mission in space exploration, given an appropriate mission.

Chiao responded at length, noting that the next phase of human space exploration is not Obama's "silly" asteroid retrieval mission, nor a vaguely defined, unfunded, one-way Mars landing, but a thorough expansion of civilization into cis-lunar space, including near and far lunar telescope bases, breakthroughs in biomedical research relating to cosmic radiation and micro-gravity, and political breakthroughs for world collaboration in space exploration. Chiao is a leading advocate of U.S.-Chinese space cooperation.

LaRouche activist Ian Overton asked Chiao how his experience at the ISS changed his concept of what is important in life. Dr. Chiao said, "I would look out the window, and see the beauty of the Earth down below. But at the same time, I knew that some places I saw, though they looked beautiful from above, were engulfed in war or hunger. And when I returned, this caused me to be far less concerned about the trifling things of life, and more concerned about what unifies us all as human beings."

A timid teenage girl in the audience, through her mother, asked how she, too, could become an astronaut. Rarely has any play, opera, or concert inspired a teenage girl to seek to become an astronaut. This power of discovery should be afforded every human being.

Gunderson's *Silent Sky* expresses a true principle of theater, and functions as a moralizing power for the nation.

Don't Criticize Obama, —Crush Him!

by Jeffrey Steinberg

Nov. 24—The November 13 terrorist attack in Paris, and the response to that attack, has now created an opportunity for Americans who are not cowards, to throw President Barack Obama from office. Beginning with the September 30 announcement by Vladimir Putin of the Russian government's decision to provide military assistance to the government of Syria, a trap has been sprung on Obama, one wherein his continued support for the ISIS terrorists has increasingly been revealed before the eyes of the entire world. Now, with the carnage and mass murder in Paris, Obama and his British masters are openly exposed as the controllers of ISIS against the nations of Europe, the very same nations who are suffering not only from the shock of the Paris attacks, but also from the rapidly escalating refugee crisis which has resulted from the Obama-British-Saudi backing of ISIS.

Presidency of the Republic of Turkey

Obama and his buddy, Turkish President Erdogan, at the Nov. 15, 2015 G20 Summit in Antalya, Turkey.

The potential for Obama's removal is very real. Nevertheless, two things must be stated: First, as discussed in the lead editorial in this issue of *EIR,* Obama is and always has been a puppet of the British monarchy, and his actions do not represent the constitutional interests of the United States. It is precisely his removal from office which is urgently required to free U.S. policy-making from British control. Without Obama's removal, there will be no real change in American policy, and the escalating crisis will quickly bring the entire world to the brink of World War III.

Second, although some few have now begun to expose some of Obama's crimes, it must be said that they usually fail even to mention his name as the criminal, much less demand his removal, and humiliate him to his face, both publicly and privately, as they must do. What's wrong with them? Are they afraid of him? Look how many people he has killed!

If there are Americans who possess courage and patriotism, they must call openly for Obama's impeachment, and demoralize him through humiliation and ridicule. Others who are straddling the fence or trying to hide, must also stop playing "practical politics" and act to save the nation. Obama's ego must be destroyed, and he must be removed now by the prescribed constitutional means—impeachment, removal under the 25th Amendment, or forced resignation.

The diagnosis of Obama as a deranged Satanist, and the demand for his removal, has been repeatedly stated by Lyndon LaRouche since 2009. The crisis we find ourselves in today is a direct result of the failure by U.S. and world leaders to act on LaRouche's warnings over the course of the last six years. In October of last year, LaRouche initiated his Manhattan Project precisely because of the worsening crisis and the lack of moral courage among the American public and its elected representatives. At last, some of the deafening silence about Obama's crimes has been broken, but far, far more is required. It is not enough to list Obama's crimes. He must be destroyed morally and removed from office.

Obama's Policies Boost ISIS

The propaganda emanating from the Obama White House concerning the war in Syria can only be described as a Bertrand Russell "snow is black" moment. Lies built upon lies. While pretending to wage war against ISIS, Obama has obediently followed the diktats of the British monarchy and has aligned the United States with the very nations that are bankrolling and arming ISIS and the other jihadist groups. The Obama Administration, under British direction, has embraced Saudi Arabia, Turkey, and Qatar, the very governments that are directing the mass murderous attacks by ISIS intended to overthrow the Bashar al-Assad government in Damascus.

Former Defense Intelligence Agency (DIA) head Gen. Michael Flynn has repeatedly emphasized that the Obama Administration has been directly arming the Syrian rebels since no later than 2012, through a weapons and personnel "rat line" running between Benghazi in Libya, and Syria, often in partnership with Turkey and Qatar. That "ratline" has been a joint project of British and American intelligence networks, under the U.S. supervision of John Brennan, the current head of the CIA who was President Obama's White House counter-terrorism czar during his first term.

Scores of DIA and State Department documents, released under the Freedom of Information Act, have detailed the depth of U.S. and British collusion with the very jihadist forces that ultimately spawned the Islamic State insurgency. In a July 29, 2015 interview with *Al Jazeera America*, Gen. Flynn dismissed the idea that Obama's policies fueled the jihadist cause as a result of "oversight." He stated that the evidence was conclusive that it was conscious White House policy to arm and back the jihadists.

When Gen. Flynn, as head of the DIA, continued to produce intelligence assessments contrary to Obama's policies, including the warning that those policies would lead to the creation of an Islamist caliphate on the eastern shores of the Mediterranean in Syria and Iraq, he was unceremoniously fired by President Obama in the summer of 2014.

Director of National Intelligence Gen. James Clapper, a slavish Obama loyalist, then began squeezing Central Command (Centcom) to alter its own assessments of the war against ISIS and al-Nusra, to paint a fake picture of success.

The Centcom intelligence fraud has now become the subject of a serious probe by the Pentagon's Inspector General (IG) and by several congressional committees, after Centcom and DIA analysts filed a formal complaint with the IG that their reports were being doctored by higher-ups. One senior military source familiar with the details of the rewriting of the Centcom assessments drew the parallel to Vice President Dick Cheney's creation of the Office of Special Plans (OSP) at the Pentagon, to produce fake intelligence about Saddam Hussein's weapons of mass destruction program, a program that in fact never existed after the 1991 Operation Desert Storm. OSP's fake allegations were used to justify the March 2003 invasion of Iraq.

Impeachment Long Overdue

The outright criminality of the Obama intervention in Syria, backing ISIS and al-Nusra terrorists while pretending to be fighting them, has already passed the constitutional threshold for initiating immediate impeachment proceedings in the House of Representatives.

Additionally, Obama's drone kill program is not only grounds for impeachment, but for criminal prosecution. The sessions every Tuesday, in which the President personally signs off on kill orders, based on intelligence dossiers cynically called "baseball cards," themselves constitute a crime of mass murder. Evidence leaked to *The Intercept* makes clear that even the minimal standards for carrying out the drone kill orders, established by the President himself, have been systematically abused, resulting in 70 to 90 percent of the people murdered in Obama's drone war being innocent bystanders.

Furthermore, to this day, Obama continues to cover up the role of the Saudi monarchy in the September 11, 2001 attacks, a coverup that directly led to the murder of U.S. Ambassador Chris Stevens and three other American personnel in Benghazi on September 11, 2012, to the Paris attacks of November 13, 2015, and many other atrocities.

Had the Saudi monarchy been brought to account for 9/11, more than a decade of support for jihadist terrorists would have been prevented. The Bush and Obama administrations' coverup of the bloody Saudi hand behind 9/11 has recurring consequences, which can no longer go unanswered in the wake of the Paris slaughter of last week.

An Outcry

Many of these crimes are coming to the surface in the dramatically changed environment since the Paris attacks.

Rep. Tulsi Gabbard (D-Hi.), an Iraq war veteran and a Vice Chair of the Democratic National Committee, has emerged as an outspoken Congressional critic of Obama's entire policy towards the Middle East and Russia. She has strongly advocated a strategic partnership with Russia to defeat the Islamic State, and has repeatedly denounced the Obama policy of regime change as one of the greatest sources of terrorist recruitment.

On November 19, Rep. Gabbard and Rep. Austin Scott (R-Ga.) introduced a bill into the House of Representatives to end the U.S. policy of attempting to overthrow the Assad government. In a press release, Gabbard said the purpose of the bill is to "bring an immediate end to the illegal, counter-productive war to overthrow the Syrian government of Assad."

Her press release listed ten reasons to end the drive to overthrow Assad, with the last reason being: "Because our war to overthrow the Assad government puts us in direct conflict with Russia and increases the likelihood of war between the United States and Russia and the possibility of another world war." She emphasized that "because the U.S. is trying to overthrow the Syrian government of Assad and Russia is supporting the government of Assad, it is impossible for us to have an effective, cooperative relationship with Russia in our mutual fight against ISIS. Our focus on overthrowing Assad is interfering with our ability to destroy ISIS."

Other members of Congress, including California Republican Dana Rohrabacher and Texas Democrat Beto O'Rourke, and GOP Presidential candidate Sen. Rand Paul (Ky.), have all assailed Obama's policy of confrontation with Russia, using the Paris atrocities to argue for strategic cooperation with Russia and the severing of ties to Saudi Arabia, which has been described as the "father of the Islamic State" for its promotion of Wahhabism.

Gen. Peter Zwack, the U.S. military attaché in Moscow from 2012 to 2014, wrote in *Defense One* on

Congresswoman Tulsi Gabbard, visiting France Nov. 20, paying her respects at the Paris memorial site where American student Nohemi Gonzalez was killed in the ISIS assault Nov. 13.

November 19 that the United States had to resume regular military-to-military relations with Russia. He called on President Obama to give a "green light" for Defense Secretary Ashton Carter and Joint Chiefs of Staff Chairman Gen. Joseph Dunford to meet with their Russian counterparts, Sergey Shoigu and Gen. Valery Gerasimov, right away.

Gen. Zwack warned, "without a dialog of any consequence our strategic defense relationship will be even more dangerous and prone to hair-trigger miscalculation or misunderstanding. Without patient dialogue, even if unsatisfying, there will be little chance of better understanding each other's perspectives and identifying points of convergence within the mud of divergence. Without contact, we both continue to demonize each other while hardening our populations. . . . Without direct dialog between our senior defense leaders we cannot even begin to consider a more mutually cooperative and secure future."

Drone Whistleblowers

Possibly what may provide the most immediate opportunity to bring down Obama altogether is the surfacing last week of four ex-Air Force drone pilots, who released a dramatic letter to President Obama, Defense Secretary Carter, and CIA Director Brennan, in which they called for an immediate end to Obama's drone kill program.

Cian Westmoreland, one of the four drone pilots who wrote to President Obama, speaking at the Taos Veterans Speak event July 11-12 in Taos, New Mexico.

"We joined the Air Force to protect American lives and to protect our Constitution. We came to the realization that the innocent civilians we were killing only fueled the feelings of hatred that ignited terrorism and groups like ISIS, while also serving as a fundamental recruitment tool similar to Guantanamo Bay. This administration and its predecessors have built a drone program that is one of the most devastating driving forces for terrorism and destabilization around the world," the four wrote.

When the guilt of our roles in facilitating this systematic loss of innocent life became too much, all of us succumbed to PTSD. We were cut loose by the same government we gave so much to—sent out in the world without adequate medical care, reliable public health services, or necessary benefits. Some of us are now homeless. Others of us barely make it.

We witnessed gross waste, mismanagement, abuses of power, and our country's leaders lying publicly about the effectiveness of the drone program. We cannot sit silently by and witness tragedies like the attacks in Paris, knowing the devastating effects the drone program has over-

seas and at home. Such silence would violate the very oaths we took to support and defend the Constitution.

The letter was signed by Staff Sergeant Brandon Bryant, Senior Airman Cian Westmoreland, Senior Airman Stephen Lewis, and Senior Airman Michael Haas.

Their story is now being broadly circulated in a documentary film that opened in New York City and Toronto last week. The eyewitness accounts they present are sufficient grounds to begin immediate impeachment proceedings against President Obama and others in the drone-kill chain of command.

Impeachment proceedings are not at all farfetched. Republican lawmakers are debating the issue behind closed doors, although the discussions are principally driven by political opportunism, rather than constitutionally informed courage.

The Obama White House is well aware of the stakes, and taking measures to defend against possible criminal charges. While pressuring the major American corporate media to black out any reference to the *Drone Papers*, Justice Department and White House lawyers are considering a range of options for protecting the President from criminal prosecution, while at the same time obligating the next administration to continue with the same drone-kill programs.

These actions by Obama's handlers show the fear that has begun to set in at the White House. The details and implications of Obama's crimes—and his British-sponsored treason—are beginning to emerge into the light of day. Nothing short of immediate impeachment or invoking of the 25th Amendment will suffice. The Obama policies of mass murder, deceit, and trading with the enemy must stop *now*.

Now is not the time for either elected officials or American citizens to be practical or to "go along to get along." The bloody victims in Paris cry out for Justice. Such justice is impossible as long as Obama occupies the White House. U.S. Senators, Representatives, and all other patriotic Americans must take their lead from LaRouche's Manhattan Project: What is required is the moral courage to accomplish his immediate removal from office. It is not enough to denounce the crimes. You must name, denounce, shame and humililate the criminal; crush his ego, and thus demoralize him to freeze his thermonuclear trigger-finger while he is quickly railroaded out of office.

THE REAL CRISIS:

It's the War, Not the Climate

by Rainer Apel, our German correspondent

Wiesbaden, Nov. 24—The contrast is as sickening as it is ironic. On the one hand, Europe is in the midst of a full mobilization, led by the Queen of England, toward the COP21 Climate Summit to convene Nov. 30 in Paris—allegedly in the interest of "saving humanity" from the threat of so-called man-made global warming, by cutting back on the very economic growth that mankind's survival requires. On the other, the tens of thousands of refugees from the Middle East and North Africa find themselves facing the threat of deportation "home" and a dramatic rise in hostility, even to the point of having arson attacks on their shelters here in Germany.

Helga Zepp-LaRouche, chairwoman of the BüSo (Civil Rights Movement Solidarity) political party, has been the only German leader to lay out the solution: Germany must immediately pull out of the British/Obama policy of regime change and war, and dump the Green agenda in favor of a full-scale embrace of the Chinese-led movement for global reconstruction through a New Silk Road. In this spirit, Zepp-LaRouche has also heartily endorsed the call by scientists Paul Driessen and Joe D'Aleo to turn the Paris Summit into a venue to mobilize to save the refugees with a real economic reconstruction plan (see below).

Germany Under the Strain

Both the political and physical situation around the refugees in Germany is reaching a breaking point.

For four months now, Germany has had a daily influx of 8-10,000 (or more) refugees entering its borders, most of them from camps in Jordan, Lebanon, Turkey, and Syria, where there are 12 *million* refugees. In November alone, the total was 180,000; by the end of the year, the numbers are expected to swell to one million or more.

These streams of refugees, which burgeoned in July, have found Germany unprepared—as Chancellor Angela Merkel herself has admitted. "Someone else should take care of that" was the attitude. Yet, in late July, Merkel took the decisive step of declaring that Germany would welcome refugees from war-torn Syria, laying aside the usual bureaucratic procedures for immigrants. That announcement was extraordinarily popular with the population at the time, as shown by the still ongoing mobilization of tens of thousands of German citizens in private groups, including churches, who have come forward to provide refugees with clothing, food, and shelter.

Merkel's humanitarian policy, however, has been compromised from the start by her kowtowing to her Finance Minister, Wolfgang Schäble, who has blocked the release of additional funds to municipalities straining to handle the refugee stream. Schäble insists that there must be zero-deficit (called the "black zero") budgeting—a mantra he has maintained toward the decaying infrastructure of Germany, as well as toward the foreign guests. The Finance Minister argues that the only way the funds can be found for the refugees is that they come from *cutting* expenditures for German citizens—a recipe bound to build up a vicious reaction.

Xenophobia on the Rise

And such a reaction has indeed come. Fed by the mainstream media trumpeting the arrival of "Merkelgate," right-wing radicals have been staging weekly demonstrations against the refugees numbering on occasions into the tens of thousands. This motion on the streets has been accompanied by in-your-face confrontations with Merkel by leading political figures, such as Christian Social Union (CSU) head Horst Seehofer, who took the occasion of his party's congress last weekend, to announce in Merkel's presence that Germany should only take in 300,000 refugees a year.

Reaping the benefits of this polarization has been the Alternative for Germany (AfD) party, a rightwing populist party which has only been on the German political scene for two years. The AfD has taken a strong anti-immigrant stance, and has seen its popularity surge

UNHCR/M. Henley

Refugees huddle up against a fence in the cold, on the border between Serbia and Croatia, on Nov. 5, 2015.

in the polls. The latest polling by the INSA group in Germany, which asked participants who they would vote for if federal elections were held today, saw the AfD rise to third place, with 10.5% of the vote. The top two vote-getters were the Christian Democrat/Christian Social Union coalition (35%) and the Social Democrats (23.5%).

The entire crisis and political debate "is like a program tailored to promote the AfD," said Mainz-based political analyst Prof. Jürgen Falter, a leading political pundit, on Nov. 19. When asked by *EIR* for her assessment of the AfD, Helga Zepp-LaRouche replied: "The AfD lacks everything: the analysis of the reasons why the refugees are fleeing South-West Asia and Africa, and the rationality needed to define a solution for the crisis. As for the German culture which they supposedly demand must be defended, I haven't found a trace of it in the AfD."

The War Policy

As Zepp-LaRouche has consistently stressed, the only way the crisis for Europe can be stopped is through a radical shift away from the geopolitical war policy of regime change which created the migration crisis to begin with. Russian President Vladimir Putin's decision to intervene militarily with the Syrian government and armed forces in the fight against ISIS terrorists, has been a giant step in this direction.

Germany's Foreign Minister Frank Walter Steinmeier was among the first in the West to respond positively. A few weeks ago, he declared that the demand for removing Syrian President Assad, as a precondition for talks among the Syrian factions, should be dropped, and a ceasefire and peace process should begin right away—with Assad's participation.

In fact, Steinmeier had already put forward a proposal for such discussions, with the inclusion of the Assad government, back in 2012.

But, as in 2012, the British and American governments have so far refused to take up collaboration with Putin, in a serious fight to destroy ISIS, and move toward a political solution in Syria. Instead of breaking with this Anglo-American war policy, Merkel decided to go along with President Obama and British Prime Minister David Cameron, and lend Germany's support to the extension of sanctions against Russia until at least July 2016. This decision was made on the sidelines of the just-concluded G20 Summit in Turkey.

There has been some sign of resistance to the war policy in the German political debate. The fact that Germany is still selling tanks and other military hardware to Saudi Arabia and Qatar, major funders of the Islamic State (Daesh), has created an outcry, as has the publicity around Germany's assistance for the war crimes being carried out in the U.S. drone warfare.

Change the Climate

Meanwhile, however, much of the political atmosphere is being absorbed with the propaganda campaign around the UN's Global Warming Summit COP21, a black propaganda torrent which even goes so far as to blame the Syrian refugees crisis on man-made climate change! No less a spokesmen for the genocidal Green agenda than Prince Charles said as much just two days ago.

While Chancellor Merkel has not gone that far, she is otherwise a strong promoter of the Global Warming hoax, and her own personal "science" advisor, Sir Franz

Joachim Schellnhuber, is set to be one of the leading stars at COP21.

Schellnhuber, who played a major role in drafting the outrageous, anti-human message of the Papal Encyclical *Laudato Si'*, is on record saying that the Earth has a carrying capacity of no more than 1 billion human beings. This is equivalent to demanding the elimination of more than six billion people—i.e. promoting genocide. Under such a mantra, the refugees might as well just go off and die.

Fortunately, there is another option, based on real science and the appropriate respect for the sacredness of human life.

Terrorism and a Cold Winter Refugee Crisis

A brutal cold spell could kill refugees. Paris COP21 delegates need to discuss **this** *climate issue.* by Paul Driessen and Joe D'Aleo*

Even after the latest Paris massacres—and previous radical Islamist atrocities in the USA, France, Britain, Canada, Spain, India, Iraq, Syria, Nigeria and elsewhere—politicians absurdly say hypothetical manmade global warming is the greatest threat facing humanity. In reality, fossil fuel contributions to climate change pose few dangers to people or planet, and winters kill 20 times more people than hot weather.

After being assured snowy winters would soon be something only read about in history books, Europe was shaken by five brutally cold winters this past decade. Thousands died, because they were homeless, lived in drafty homes with poor heating systems, or could not afford adequate fuel.

It could happen again, with even worse consequences. "Millions of desperate people are on the march," Walter Russell Mead recently wrote in the *Wall Street Journal*. "Sunni refugees driven out by the barbarity of the Assad regime in Syria, Christians and Ya-

zidis fleeing the pornographic violence of Islamic State, millions more of all faiths and no faith fleeing poverty and oppression without end."

Where are they heading? Mostly not into neighboring Arab countries, most of which have yanked their welcome mats. Instead, if they're not staying in Turkey, they're going north to Europe—into the path the extremely cold Siberian Express has increasingly taken. Germany alone could face the challenge of feeding and sheltering 800,000 to 1,000,000 freezing refugees this winter.

Cold Kills

If a blast of frigid Siberian air should hit, temperatures in parts of eastern and northern Europe and the western Former Soviet Union could become 70 degrees F (39C) colder than cold spells in much of the Middle East. During the coldest Siberian outbreaks, it gets as lethally cold as -40F (-40C).

Northern and eastern Europeans are largely acclimated to such cold. However, for refugees from regions where winters average 20 to 30 degrees warmer, makeshift houses or tents will make their sojourn a bone-chilling experience. Europe's exorbitant energy costs, resulting from its obeisance to climate chaos credos, could make this an even worse humanitarian crisis.

However, to listen to the UN, many world leaders, environmental NGOs, scientists from the climate alarm industry, and their sycophant media—especially on the eve of their Paris 2015 global warming summit—threats from cold weather are not supposed to happen. Just 15 years ago, the German magazine *Spiegel* proclaimed, "Good-bye winter: In Germany bitter cold winters are now a thing of the past." That same year, a British Climate Research Unit scientist said "children aren't going to know what snow is."

The media dutifully repeated similar claims each year, until unbelievably cold, snowy winters began hitting in 2008/09. In December 2010, England had its second-coldest December since 1659, amid the Little Ice Age. For five years, 2008-2013, snow paralyzed travel in England and northern and western Europe. Not surprisingly, the same media then blamed manmade global warming for the harsh winters.

In reality, natural Atlantic Ocean cycles lasting around 60 years control winter temperatures in Europe and Eastern North America. When the North Atlantic warms, "blocking high pressure systems" largely pre-

* Joe D'Aleo is a Certified Consulting Meteorologist and American Meteorological Society Fellow and co-founder of The Weather Channel. Paul Driessen is senior policy analyst for the Committee For A Constructive Tomorrow. Climate experts Allan MacRae and Madhav Khandekar contributed to this article. This article first appeared on www.icecap.us

creative commons/Anthony Appleyard

Five of the last 10 winters in Europe have been subject to frigid Siberian weather. Here, Manchester, England on Jan. 5, 2010 during one of the worst such spells.

vent warm Atlantic air from reaching Europe.

There is also a strong correlation between the sun's geomagnetic activity and these blocking-induced cold winters in Europe. The five brutally cold winters ending in 2012/13 had the lowest level of solar geomagnetic activity in the entire record, dating back some 90 years.

When the North Atlantic is warm and the sun's geomagnetic patterns are weak, these blocking patterns keep warmer Atlantic air out of Europe. Frigid air from off deep snows in Siberia can then more easily invade from the east, bringing sub-zero cold and heavy snows. That's what happened from 2008 to 2013.

The ocean and solar factors eased in 2013, and the last two years have seen more Atlantic air and milder winters. However both solar and ocean patterns are starting to return to the situation where cold invasions are more likely. That could usher in nasty surprises for the Middle Eastern refugees.

Even this year's early winter October cold brought news stories about Syrian children becoming sick amid exposure to colder weather than they were used to. In Austria, adults and children alike were already complaining about the weather and wishing they could go home.

In fact, cold weather kills 20 times more people than hot weather, according to a *Lancet* medical journal study that analyzed 74 million deaths in 384 locations across 13 countries. It should be required reading for the 40,000-plus bureaucrats, politicians, activists and promoters who will soon descend on Paris, to enjoy five-star hotels and restaurants while blathering endlessly about dire threats of global warming.

They should ponder the fact that the *Lancet* study reflects normal societies in peaceful countries. Even there, many more people die each year during the four winter months than in the eight non-winter months. Indeed, even the United States experiences some 100,000 Excess Winter Deaths per year.

In the United Kingdom, the winter death rate is about twice as high as in the USA: excess winter deaths range up to 50,000 per year—due to the UK's poorer home insulation and heating systems, and much higher energy costs caused by its climate and renewable energy policies.

The refugees' excess winter death toll could well be even greater, due to the high cost of European energy and the migrants' extreme poverty, poor nutrition, inadequate clothing and blankets, pre-existing diseases, and makeshift housing: tents, trailers and other dwellings that have little or no insulation or central heat.

Change the Paris Agenda!

Systematic misinformation about the dangers of fossil fuels and hot versus cold weather has helped make this crisis much worse than needs be. Climate alarmists will thus bear the blame for thousands of avoidable deaths among refugees this winter, especially if the Siberian Express invades once again.

The Paris climate conferees need to focus on humanity's real and immediate dangers: this rapidly growing refugee crisis, abysmal EU economies and job losses, and the billions worldwide who still lack the adequate, reliable, affordable energy required to end their crushing poverty, malnutrition, disease and early death, by ensuring clean water, proper sanitation, modern hospitals, lights, refrigerators and plentiful food. The climate conferees must address the following much more pressing questions.

How is climate change more important than safeguarding refugees who are already suffering from cold weather? Should conferees be focused on hypothetical future manmade climate chaos, while EU nations squabble over who will take how many refugees and potential terrorists, amid a possible winter crisis? What contingency plans do they have for another bout of frigid weather possibly invading the continent?

When a million refugees are freezing in squalid conditions with inadequate shelter, food, heat, clothing and medical care, and 1.3 billion people still do not have electricity, why would the world commit to spending billions on alleged future global warming catastrophes? As Bjorn Lomborg puts it, why would the world also want to give up *nearly $1 trillion in GDP* every year for the rest of this century, to avert a total hypothetical (computer modeled) temperature rise of just 0.306 degrees C (0.558 F) by 2100?

Where will the money come from to combat growing war and terrorism, aid the millions displaced by these horrors, rebuild devastated cities, put millions of people back to work, and bring electricity and better lives to billions of others—if we continue this obsession over global warming? Do humans really play a big enough role in climate change to justify these incomprehensible price tags? Where is the actual evidence? Not computer models or press releases—the actual evidence?

It would be an unconscionable crime against humanity, if the nations gathering in Paris implement policies to protect our planet's energy-deprived masses from hypothetical manmade climate disasters decades from now, by perpetuating poverty and disease that kill millions more people tomorrow.

These are the real reasons climate change is a critical moral issue. We need to recognize that, and stop playing games with people's lives. We must acknowledge that horrific computer model scenarios do not reflect planetary reality—and must not guide energy policy.

The Islamic Renaissance Was a Dialogue of Civilizations

by Hussein Askary

The purpose of this report is not to indulge in theological discussions, nor plans for social reforms in Muslim countries, although these are necessary matters that have to be taken seriously by political and religious leaders of these nations themselves. The purpose is to encourage both Muslims and non-Muslims to investigate and find inspiration in the great Golden Age of the Islamic Renaissance to solve today's dilemmas. Although I am Muslim by faith, I believe in a secular society, living in a modern nation-state where freedom of faith is granted for all. In modern times, the use of religion for political purposes or turning politics into a shadow of religion are recipes for disaster.

Nov. 23—The Muslim nations and the world have been captured by a terrible state of chaos, bloodshed, and insanity. The terrorist attacks in Paris on November 13, like those attacks which have actually become almost a daily occurrence in large parts of Southwest Asia and North Africa, carried out by people who claim to be fighting for the Islamic faith and "Muslim Ummah" (collective name for all Muslim peoples), have brought the world closer to a global religious war.

In reality, the overwhelming majority of the victims of the so-called Islamist terror groups such as the Islamic State in Iraq and the Levant (ISIL), al-Qaeda, and others, are themselves Muslims. "Islam has been hijacked," is a common statement uttered by Muslims all over the world who disapprove of and condemn what these terrorist organizations are perpetrating in the name of Islam. In the West, the words Islam and Muslim are increasingly being associated with war and terrorism.

But the world today cannot afford to fall into the same trap that brought upon human civilization such calamities as the Crusades of 1099-1291, which, together with the Mongol invasions, resulted in the Global Dark Age; nor the religious wars of Europe from 1492, which did not stop until the 1648 signing of the Treaty of Westphalia. In order to prevent that, there are certain issues that have to be resolved immediately:

1. What is source of the current crisis;

2. What is the aim of its creators; and

3. How it can be stopped, so that the world and humankind, with the participation of Muslims as citizens of their respective nations, could take a new leap in the process of evolution.

We have to figure out what kind of ideas can inspire whole generations of Muslims and non-Muslims, who are either direct victims of these religious wars, or who, under the pressure of the destruction of their nations by illegal wars, economic sanctions, and geopolitical manipulations, could potentially be the recruits for such destructive forces as IS and al-Qaeda, for example.

There are clearly subjective causes from within the Muslim societies themselves that have to be critically discussed and corrected. But we should not fool ourselves that this by itself would transform the world. The current world order, dominated by the trans-Atlantic powers, itself is the key source of this crisis, and has to be stopped and changed.

The Key to the Crisis

This "dis-order" has brought to the world the "jihadist" militancy that was created by the Anglo-American-Saudi intelligence services in the Afghan war 1980-1989, the Anglo-Saudi attacks of 9/11 on the United States, the invasion and destruction of Iraq in 2003, and of Libya in 2011, and the current horrendous war on Syria fomented and backed by such allies of the United States, Britain and the EU, as Saudi Arabia, Turkey, and Qatar. It is here that the key to the current crisis lies.

This tool of geopolitics has now turned into a plague that is threatening all civilization with its nihilistic and satanic view of man as a blood-thirsty beast. The "pragmatic" use of these bestial tools, unfortunately continues today in the region. The same goes for the destabilization of Russia through Chechen rebels, and China through the Uighur militants, both of whom are now actively involved in the war in Syria against the government in Damascus and in support of ISIL and the al-Nusra Front (al-Qaeda) and other terrorist groups, who have hijacked the name of Islam and turned it to something completely opposite to what it really was in the Islamic Renaissance era.

The ideology of the "Clash of Civilizations," of such Anglo-American ideo-

Dept. of Defense

Two key representatives of the "disorder:" Former Vice President Dick Cheney and then-Crown Prince Sultan of Saudi Arabia, meeting in 1990.

logues as Samuel Huntington and Bernard Lewis, falls into the same bestial category. Their claim that China, the Islamic world, and the West will inevitably clash, and cannot co-exist as equals and work together for economic, scientific and cultural development, is debunked by the Renaissance efforts illustrated below.

The reality of Muslim society between the Eighth and Thirteenth Centuries was not always rosy and fine. Civil wars, bloody power struggles and intrigues were a normal state of affairs. However, most of those in power and their scholars, advisers, scientists, and citizens, realized and agreed that *knowledge was power*. Today, the Islamic world has been pulled down into a bloody political and religious struggle, but knowledge and the love of wisdom have taken a back seat. Many Muslim nations today are experiencing a state of cultural and economic stagnation, if not outright degeneration.

What is common between the Western bestial ideologues and politicians such as Dick Cheney and Tony Blair, with their counterparts in Saudi Arabia, ISIL and al-Qaeda, is the process of dehumanization of individuals and groups. It is no coincidence that many of the top Iraqi military leaders of ISIL, are former Iraqi soldiers and officers of the Republican Guard and special forces, who after the invasion of Iraq in 2003, were imprisoned and tortured by U.S. and British forces in the most un-

imaginable and humiliating way in such infamous locations as Abu Ghraib prison and Camp Bucca. That is where the leader of ISIL, Abu Bakr al-Baghdadi himself, was incarcerated by the U.S. forces in Iraq in 2004.

These prisons, like other CIA-run prisons around the globe, became the recruiting and brainwashing centers that produced a new generation of mass-killers, who, exactly like their prison-guards and torturers, regarded anyone who was not on their side as less than human, and more like an animal or an insect who could be crushed, maimed or burned in cold blood. Intolerance is the key aspect of this bestial mentality.

This mentality does have precedents in Islamic history, in such theologians as the Fourteenth-Century Ibn Taymiyyah, who is the key source of inspiration for the Saudi Wahhabi movement and its creations, al-Qaeda and ISIL (see appendix).

What Image of Man?

After a long period of development, in what can be called the Golden Age of Islamic civilization (Eighth-Thirteenth Centuries), eastern Islamic civilization went into a prolonged dark age after the first destruction of Baghdad by the Mongol hordes in 1258. The Muslim regions did not recover until after World War II. That Dark Age swept over central Asia, Iran, Iraq, and the Levant, and Turkey. Egypt and North Africa were also

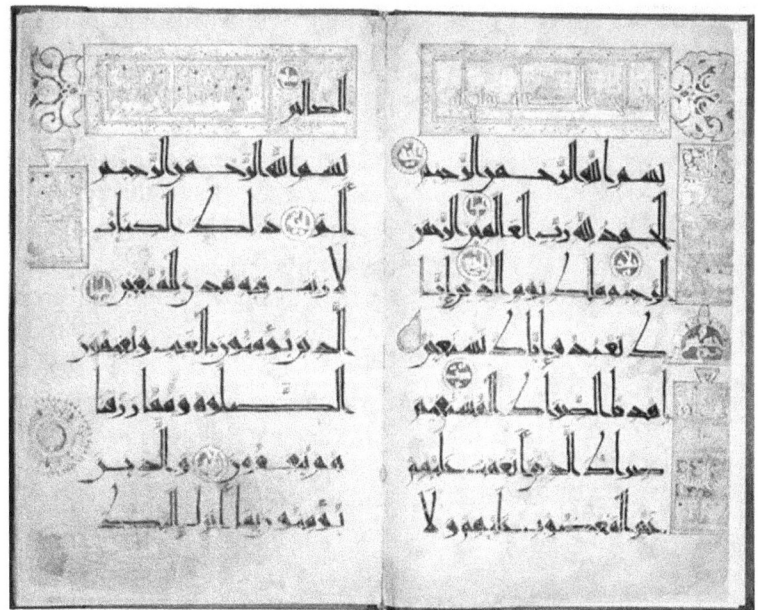

Manuscript of the Quran *in color and gold on paper. This fragment contains the surah al-Fatihah (the Opening) and al-Baqarah (the Calf).*

deeply affected by this process. Islamic Civilization survived in Al-Andalus (Spain) a little longer, until 1492.

If the world survives the current crisis, with the combined efforts of the BRICS nations and wise people in the West, the Muslim world will have to reflect on its history and purpose of existence, and on the brightest periods and aspects of its heritage in order to muster the cultural and moral strength that it has lost for both subjective and objective reasons.

The image of man in the *Quran* is no different from that in Christianity or Judaism. Human beings are creatures with special characteristics that separate them from all other creatures, by the merit of being created "in the image of God" as in Judeo-Christian belief, or "having Allah blow His own Soul unto Adam" (Surat al-Hijr, 15:29 *Holy Quran*). Humankind also inherited dominion over the Earth (Surat al-Baqara 2:30 *Holy Quran*), as the Creator's creative representative on Earth, to whom the Creator himself had taught all existing knowledge (2:31 *Holy Quran*), and mankind is commanded to develop it.

From the very outset of the message of Islam, the Prophet Mohammed and the "Revelation" of the *Quran* emphasized the importance of reading or recitation. "Iqra'a," [read, recite or proclaim] was, according to Islamic traditions, the first command Mohammad received through the "Revelation's" Archangel Jibril (Gabriel). In a truly Promethean spirit, The Prophet Mohammed reportedly received these words:

1. Read in the name of thy Lord, who created-

2. Created man out of a leech-like clot.

3. Read/Proclaim: And thy Lord is Most Bountiful,-

4. He Who taught the use of the Pen.

5. Taught man that which he knew not. (Surat al-'Alaq or verse No. 96, the *Holy Quran*).

There is also a saying/tradition (Hadith) attributed to the Prophet Mohammad—whose authenticity some dispute, but which is widely spread even in early Islamic books—which says: "Seek knowledge even if it were in China! Seeking knowledge is a duty upon each Muslim." This is a significant sign of the early Islamic society's emphasis on seeking knowledge and wisdom, which is the root cause of the massive cultural, scientific, and economic evolution that took place in the Islamic "empire" in those centuries.

It is well-known that the Prophet Mohammad was a merchant who travelled for 25 years of his early life to Yemen from Mecca in the Winter to meet merchants from Asia and East Africa, and to Syria in the Summer to meet with merchants from the Levant, Persia, and Rome,—and even those from India and China who had come through the Silk Road. His knowledge of the traditions and cultures of these peoples is reflected in the *Quran* and Hadith (tradition). The emphasis on a knowledge-based society was one key cause of the Islamic Renaissance. Another was the recognition of the universality of knowledge, which enabled the Muslims to assimilate enormous bodies of knowledge from every possible culture they came in contact with, without any prejudice. Therefore, they could bring together the sciences, philosophy, technology, etc., from China, India, Persia, Greece, and Africa, into one melting pot and institution.

The reference to China was not a mere metaphor. Diplomatic relations with China were established less than twenty years after the Prophet Mohammad's death. His companion Saad ibn Abi-Waqqas visited the Chinese Tang Dynasty Emperor in 650. The Chinese Emperor Yung-Wei, according to writer Yusuf Abdul Rahman, "respected the teachings of Islam and

FIGURE 1

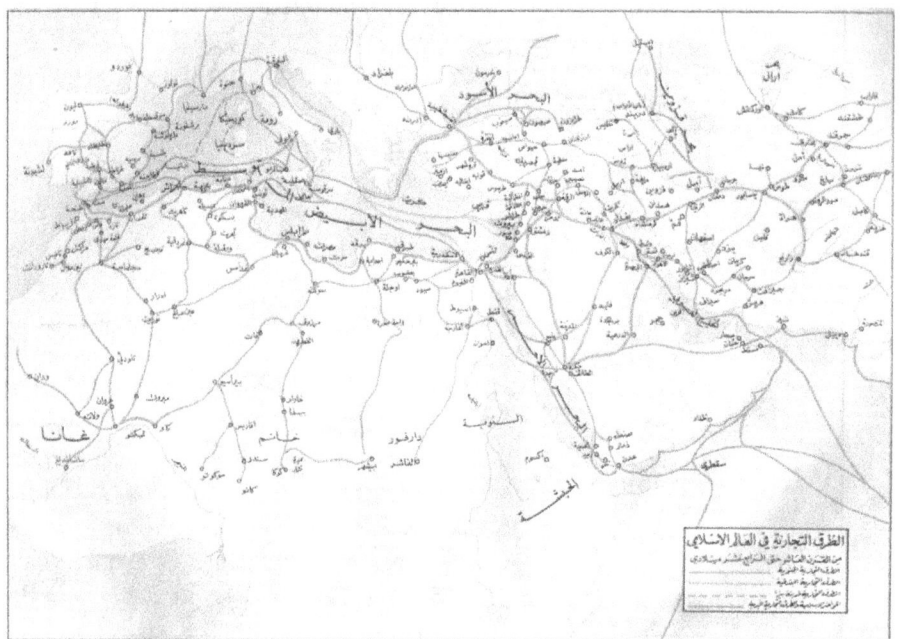

Map of trade routes in the Islamic World between the Tenth and Fourteenth Centuries. The density of large cities along the trade routes are a confirmation that trade is a byproduct of development.

considered it to be compatible with the teachings of Confucius." To show his admiration of Islam, the Emperor approved the establishment of China's first mosque, reportedly Huaisheng Mosque in Guangzhou. That mosque still stands there today. Although the story of the visit by Waqqas is not firmly documented, the evidence is that the mosque was built in the Seventh Century.

The Silk Road: An Ancient Image of the Future

There is an intimate, intertwined relationship between the Ancient Silk Road and Islamic Civilization and its dialogue with East and West. Fortunately, once again, today the emergence of the New Silk Road strategy, which is spearheaded by China and also its allies in the BRICS constellation, Russia and India, gives hope for reversing this spiral of violence and destruction. Rather than the Clash of Civilizations, a "Dialogue of Civilizations" can be pursued, as former Iranian President Mohammad Khatami phrased it, or a harmony of interests among nations, and what President Xi Jinping has called a "Win-Win" strategy.

The Ancient Silk Road, and indeed the New Silk Road, have to be regarded as vehicles of civilization-building. As Helga Zepp-LaRouche, the Chairwoman

of the Schiller Institute (and the "Silk Road Lady" as she is now known in China), has repeatedly emphasized, and as my colleagues at *Executive Intelligence Review* and I have illustrated the concept of the "Development Corridor,"—the New Silk Road is not about the transfer of merchandise from point A in the East to point B in the West or *vice versa*. The same goes for the ancient Silk Road.

Rather, the Silk Road is a vehicle for scientific, technological and cultural exchange, and a means to bring new tools to the peoples along the route between A and B to improve their productivity, their creativity, and thus their standards of living. That, in turn, enables them to use their specific local or national culture and creativity to invent and create new tools to give back to the other societies along the same route.

Incorporating New Technologies

What Muslim society did from the Eighth to the Thirteenth Centuries, with certain ups and downs, with the Chinese technology to produce paper from wood pulp and other cellulose fibers, is one of the brightest examples of this cultural transformation process.

In real economics, i.e. physical economics as Lyndon LaRouche has taught, one of the key metrics of economy is to figure out how the introduction of a new technology or scientific principle into one part of the economic process, increases the productivity of the system as a whole. Paper-making is one such technology, whose dissemination (through Islamic societies) across three continents, created such massive effects on human society, that it will take many years and many experts to measure its impact on the productivity of the human society throughout the past eleven centuries.

Arabic was also the *lingua franca* from the Eighth to the Fifteenth Centuries, from Central Asia all the way through Southwest Asia and North Africa to Spain. The introduction of paper from China to this vast transcontinental culture, made the further assimilation and spreading of knowledge easier, cheaper and faster by orders of magnitude.

The history of the invention and dissemination of paper is a wonderful story of how Chinese, Indian, Persian, Arab, and European cultures collaborated directly or indirectly to elevate the human base of knowledge, culture and economy.[1]

The advantages of paper are that it is flexible, absorbs ink more efficiently, is light in weight and costs less. Government bureaucrats in the Islamic empire realized that texts and seals written or impressed on paper were very difficult to remove or forge. Merchants on the Silk Road preferred paper letters of credit and checks to gold and silver coins which were a security risk.

Another important characteristic is that paper can be produced anywhere in the world, no matter the climate or geography. What is needed is cellulose, which is the most abundant of all naturally occurring organic compounds, and fresh water both for the production process and also for water wheels to power papermills. In Central Asia, Iraq, eastern Syria and Egypt, all these elements were available, and helped establish the largest paper mills in the world between the Eighth and Thirteenth Centuries.

Islam and the Tang Dynasty: A Clash Produces a New Culture

The Tang Dynasty in China reached its pinnacle of prosperity, but also of political and military expansion in the late Seventh Century AD up to the middle of the Eighth Century, which was considered the Golden Age of the empire. Its capital Chang'an (currently Xi'an) was the most populous city in the world, with around 800,000 to 1 million inhabitants in the 760s. The total population of China was estimated to be about 50 million.

This factor enabled the dynasty to build a massive army, which managed to expand the influence of the empire westward into the Turkic steppe in Central Asia, dominating and benefitting from the trade on the Silk Road. Many minor kingdoms and cities paid tribute to the Tang Emperor, and provided wealth from the fertile Ferghana Valley, watered by the Syr Darya River which is today shared by Kyrgyzstan, Uzbekistan, and Tajikistan.

1. 1. Bloom, Jonathan M., *Paper before Print, The History and Impact of Paper in the Islamic World*, Yale University Press, 2001.

FIGURE 2

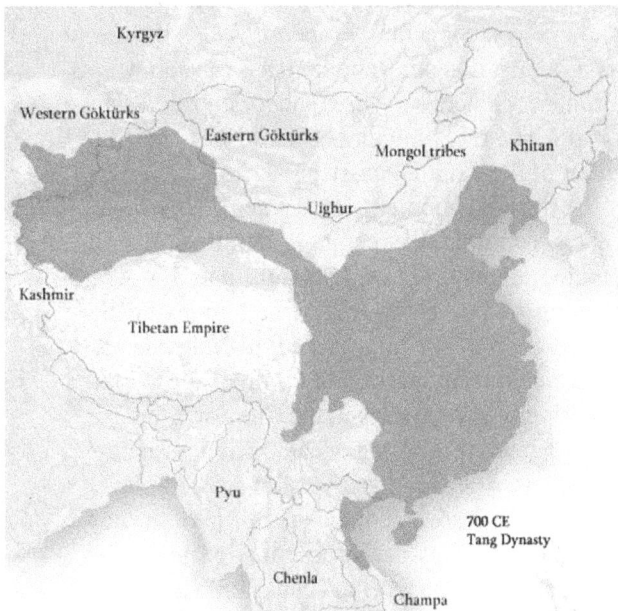

The Chinese Tang Dynasty expansion, AD 750.

Simultaneously, the Islamic Umayyad Caliphate (660-750 AD) had likewise expanded both westward throughout North Africa into the Iberian Peninsula and eastward all the way to Transoxania (i.e. beyond the Oxus River). With the emergence of the Abbasid Dynasty, which overthrew the Umayyads in 750 AD, the Islamic and Chinese empires collided face-to-face in that region. A major battle, the Battle of Talas in the valley of the Talas River (in today's north-eastern Kyrgyzstan) took place in July 751, in which the huge Chinese army was defeated with great losses. It is reported, although not confirmed, that thousands of Chinese prisoners were taken into custody by the Muslims, including many craftsmen, including "papermaking artisans."

The Battle of Talas put an end to the westward expansion of the Tang Dynasty. But, interestingly, both empires were interested in continuing the commercial process along the Silk Road, and also in security cooperation, as both sides viewed the local Turkic tribes as a threat, in the border region between the two empires. According to the Chinese-Muslim historian Bai Shouyi, diplomatic missions and gift exchanges continued, with thirteen missions between 752 and 798.

An Lushan Rebellion, a Turning Point

However, the most dramatic development that brought China and the Islamic world closer, was the assistance delivered by the Muslim Caliph Abu Jaafar al-Mansour (founder and builder of Baghdad in 767) to the Tang Emperor to face the devastating An Lushan Rebellion. An Lushan was a Chinese General of Sogdian (Central Asian) origin. The rebellion that began in 755, ended in favor of the Tang Dynasty in 763.

A decisive moment came when An Lushan's rebels captured the capital Chang'an in 756, forcing many of its inhabitants and Emperor Suzong to flee eastward. At that moment, the Emperor Suzong approached al-Mansour for help, and the latter sent 5,000 Arab troops (some reports say 25,000), to aid the Chinese Emperor. They helped recapture the capital and push back the rebels. Many of these Muslim soldiers stayed in China, and are said to be the origin of the current Hui Muslims of China. Muslim merchants also continued to travel to China, and the spreading of teachings was tolerated at that time by the Confucian-influenced Tang Emperors.

This collaboration led to closer cultural exchanges, which spurred the scientific and cultural revolution that became the Islamic Renaissance.

The Baghdad Renaissance

During the reign of Haroun al-Rashid's son, Caliph al-Ma'mun (reigned 813-833), Baghdad was transformed into the global scientific and philosophical "research center." Any important scientific or philosophical manuscript from any part of the world and in any language, would have found its way to the House of Wisdom established in Baghdad by al-Ma'mun. There, it would be translated, studied, copied, replicated (if it was a discovery or experiment) and disseminated without restrictions. This is a wholly major history in itself, which I dealt with in my report "Baghdad 767-1258 A.D.: Melting Pot for a Universal Renaissance," (*EIR*, October 18, 2013.)

The trans-cultural dialog and enrichment achieved in sciences, music, and philosophy, in addition to economic activities such as architecture, hydraulics, and navigation through new modes of cartography, reached completely breathtaking levels in this era, facilitated by the introduction of papermaking from China and the expansion of the Silk Road.

Greek geometry and mathematics were fused with the Indian numbering system (so-called Arab numer-

Maqamat al-Hariri Library, illustration by Yahya al-Wasiti, Baghdad 1237
Scholars in an Abbasid library.

als) in the House of Wisdom by Mohammad ibn Musa al-Khawarizmi (Latinized as Algoritmi), the father of algebra, whose name is immortalized today in the term *algorithms*. Greek and Persian books of medicine were translated and developed into a whole new system of medical education by such scientists as Abu Ali Ibn Sina (Avicenna) whose book *Al-Qanun fil Tib* (The Canon of Medicine completed in 1025) was the main medical textbook throughout the Islamic world and even in Medieval Europe for centuries. The art of composing terrestrial and celestial spherical cartography, incorporating Greek and Chinese methods, was refined and spread from Baghdad into many parts of the world.

The most important aspect of this massive development is that it was done as joint projects of many cultures, religions, and nations without any prejudice. Ibn Sina was Persian, Al-Khawarizmi was Turkish, and Qusta ibn Luqa, the most important translator of Greek and Latin manuscripts in the House of Wisdom, was a Melkite Christian of Greek extraction. But they all worked in Baghdad and spoke Arabic. One of the most amusing ironies in this regard is that the man who first codified and compiled all Arabic grammar in one book *Al-Kitab*, was Sibawayh (665-696), who was a Persian.

Sibawayh (whose name mean "the smell of apple" in Farsi) was born in Persia, but when he was still a child, his family moved to Basrah, in Iraq. He later moved to Baghdad to join the flourishing scientific society there. His teacher in Basrah was Al-Khalil al-Farahidi, a musician and linguist who was the first to codify and write down the entire metrical system of Arabic poetry, and who also wrote books on phonetics and articulation.

The largest Abbasid library was built in Baghdad in 991 by a Persian minister under Caliph Baha-ul-Dawla, named Sabur ibn Ardashir. It contained over 10,000 volumes on a range of scientific subjects. However, it was in Spain that the greatest of all libraries was built, in Cordoba, during the reign of Caliph al-Hakam II (reigned 961-76), a descendant of the Umayyads. Al-Hakam's main interest was books, and he started collecting books in his teens and was tutored by the best scholars of the time. Al-Hakam's library contained 400,000 books. The catalogue of titles alone is said to have filled 44 volumes. Scholar Jonathan Bloom says that even if these numbers are exaggerated, "still, at even one-tenth the size, [it] would have been larger, by a factor of fifty or more, than any library in Christendom." Furthermore, this library in Cordoba, and those in Toledo, were available for outsiders too. Muslim, Jewish, and Christian scholars, astronomers, physicians, and theologians, would meet in special reading and meeting rooms in the library to discuss and debate. Later, in Fatimid Egypt (Tenth-Eleventh Centuries), a similar library was built, modelled on the one in Baghdad, and almost as large as the one in Cordoba.

Economic Impact

Many of the scientific discoveries that were made in the scientific institutions were also incorporated in the economic development of society. Providing water to the cities and agricultural lands required massive infrastructure projects, such as canals, water wheels, hydraulic systems for lifting and transporting water to the cities, etc. Scientists like the Banu Musa brothers, who lived and worked in the House of Wisdom in Baghdad, designed many machines for water pumping and transportation. Their works were transcribed and published in books. Facilitated by the availability of paper in the Islamic lands was the spread of other arts,—metalworking, ceramics, and particularly textiles,—"for art-

EIRNS/Michael Weissbach

Interior of the Great Mosque of Cordoba, built A.D. 786-787 by 'Abd al-Rahman I.

ists could create designs on paper that artisans could apply to their work." This was most efficiently used in architecture, because the repetition of patterns, which is characteristic of Islamic architecture, could be transmitted through pattern books.

Commerce, which had developed massively due to agricultural and industrial development during the early centuries of Islam, thrived. The Islamic world from the Indus and Central Asia to the Pyrenees in Europe, was one "common market." Merchants travelling long distances with their commodities, preferred not to carry gold or silver coins as they travelled. Paper credit, such as letters of credit (*Suftaja*) and checks (originating from the Persian *Sakka* or Arabic *Sakk*), were widely used in the trading centers of the Silk Road, and in Africa and the Mediterranean. Copies of these were found among the Geniza Papers, referring to the late Nineteenth Century discovery made in the Genizah (Hebrew for storage room) of the Ben Ezra Synagogue in Old Cairo, Egypt, of a collection of almost 300,000 manuscripts.

Transmission to Europe

In addition to Greek philosophy and science, translated back from Arabic books, it was mostly from Islamic Spain that Europeans learned about the advances of the Islamic Renaissance.

Unlike the Byzantine Christians, the Spanish and French Christians had a different view of Islam and Arabic altogether. More important, Christian theologians began an effort to translate Arabic books. Peter the Venerable, abbot of the Benedictine monastery at Cluny, France, travelled to Spain for several years and returned in 1141. Peter commissioned the translation of at least five major books, including the *Quran*, from Arabic to Latin.

Another very important character in the Islamic-Christian dialog was Ramon Llull (Latin: Raymundus Lullus). He was born in 1231 in Palma, Majorca, which was under the control of the Christian Kingdom of Aragon. He travelled in Muslim Spain and North Africa, and learned Arabic to study and translate the works of Arab theologians and philosophers. Although Peter's mission was intended to refute Islam's "heresies," and Llull's was to convert Muslims to Christianity, they both shifted the European critique of Islam from looking at it from outside, into studying it from inside through translating and reading the original works.

Inspired by Francis of Assisi, Llull came to the conclusion that Muslims, Jews, and Christians believe in the same "attributes" of God the Creator, and that Muslims should be approached by reasoning and dialog, and not by the force of weapons. Cardinal Nicholas of Cusa later made the same arguments in his 1453 groundbreaking book *De Pace Fidei* (On the Peace of Faith), shortly after the Ottomans invaded Constantinople. Llull had argued for the importance of linguistic education at the major universities in Europe. It was partly due to his influence that the Council of Vienne ordered the creation of chairs of Hebrew, Arabic, and Chaldean (Aramaic) at the universities of Bologna, Oxford, Paris, and Salamanca, as well as at the Papal Court.

The story of the Islamic Renaissance should be a source of inspiration for all those who, while fighting against the bestiality of such satanic forces as ISIL and their masters, and fighting to establish peace, are at the same time thinking about the future of their societies and nations. How would a world of obviously different cultures, religions, and traditions come together to create something common, beautiful and great?

As Lyndon LaRouche described the matter with associates recently, an educated society is one where, even though the great majority may not be geniuses themselves, the society has certain qualifying intellectual and moral capabilities, and they do know that they must look up to the geniuses of history and of our own day, and walk on their path. The greatest Muslims of the Renaissance period, looked to the great geniuses of other cultures, like the Greeks, and learned from them,—but in that process produced their own geniuses. We should all look up to them and walk upon their path.

Wahhabism and Ash'arism

The highest Wahhabi religious personality in Saudi Arabia, the Mufti and Chairman of the Supreme Council of Ulama (clergy), Abdul-Aziz bin Abdullah al-Asheikh, on March 12, 2012 described the acts of fundraising and supporting the rebel Free Syrian Army as *jihad* under Islamic law, because, according to him, the Syrian regime is *kafir* (blasphemous or apostate). However, when it came to peaceful protests in Saudi Arabia by those demanding economic and political justice, these he declared to be evil.

This is a typical example of the selectiveness of the Wahhabi clergy, which always takes the side of the House of Saud. A former Mufti, Abdul Aziz bin Baz, was asked about Muslims wearing crosses and other ornaments; he declared it a sin. However, when he was asked about King Fahd wearing the Iron Cross of the British Empire, awarded to him by Queen Elizabeth II, making him an honorary British Knight in 1987, bin Baz replied that "if the Wali al-Amr (the ruler of Muslims) considers that wearing the cross has a benefit to the Muslim nation, then that cannot be considered an offense"!

This idea that the "ruler of the Muslim nation" cannot be faulted was an artificial creation of theologians who were used by Umayyad kings at the beginning of the Eighth Century to get immunity for oppressing the people and killing Muslim opponents, to acquire and preserve power. They manipulated the following verses from the *Quran* as a blank check for their rule: "O you who have believed, obey Allah and obey the Messenger and those in authority among you" (Surah Al-Nisaa, verse 59).

Al-Ash'ari

One of the most vocal such theologians was **Abu al-Hasan al-Ash'ari** (875-935), the spearhead against the Islamic Renaissance. His concept was that Allah is the Creator of everything in existence, and so both evil and good acts of human beings are predestined by God's will. Therefore, the evil committed by the ruler is not his own creation, but that of God, and if people tried to change that evil, they would be committing a sin against God's will!

This view was the opposite of the school of Mu'tazila, which called for a rational method of interpretation of the *Quran*, and argued that the divine injunctions of the Creator are accessible to human reason, and that reason must be the ultimate criterion for judging good and evil.

Al-Ash'ari, who started as a student of the Mu'tazilites, turned against them in 912, and published his book *Clarification of the Bases of Religion*, in which he argued for absolutely literal interpretation of the *Quran*, in a clear attack on the Mu'tazilites. The Mu'tazilites had become a strong philosophical and scientific school in the early Renaissance age in Basrah and Baghdad in the Eighth Century.

Al-Ash'ari attacked, for example, their view that God's references to his "seeing, hearing, having hands, 'sitting on the throne,' etc." were metaphors. He claimed that God does indeed have such physical attributes, because that is what is stated in the *Quran*.

As part of the Seljuk power grab in Baghdad, **Nizam-ul Mulk al-Tusi** (1018-92), the Seljuk vizir (minister) under Sultan Alp Arsalan, raised the Ash'arites to prominence in Baghdad to take over the Shafi'i Sunni sect, while undermining the other Sunni sects, creating sectarian strife in Baghdad. He established the Nizamiya school of theology, the institution from which a later theologian emerged, **Abu Hamid al-Ghazali** (1111-58), who launched the final and most fatal attack on the science and philosophy of the Islamic Renaissance.

His book, *The Destruction of Philosophers*, is entirely oriented to destroying the philosophical thoughts of Ibn Sina (980-1037), the greatest of Muslim scientists and philosophers of the Islamic Renaissance, and his predecessor al-Farabi. Al-Ghazali's inquisition became a tool of destruction of rational thinking, pushing society into mystical fundamentalism. The socially and economically weakened and divided Islamic state became an easy prey for the Venetian-run Crusades, and later, the Mongol invasion.

Ibn Taymiyyah

Taqi al-Din Ibn Taymiyyah, who was born under the Mongol occupation in 1263 in Harran (now southern Turkey), has today become the key theological source of the Wahhabi, Salafi, and jihadist takfiri groups. Ibn Taymiyyah was the source of inspiration of Abdul-Wahhab, such Egyptian Muslim Brotherhood founders as Sayyid Qutb and Hassan al-Banna, and later the Afghan Mujahideen main preacher Abdullah Azzam, and Osama bin Laden. Not only did he preach the extreme literal interpretation of the *Quran*, but also became a Fatwa factory for armed groups and political leaders of his time who were willing to use him in their power struggle.

He preached complete non-toleration of Christians and Jews, and using public executions and maiming for the smallest criticism of the religion or suspicion of heresy. He declared many Muslim sects as worse than the infidels, such as the Alawites and Shia, saying they should be completely eliminated from the face of Earth. Many leaders of ISIL, al-Qaeda, al-Nusra and such "moderate" Syrian rebel groups as Army of Islam, use his fatwas against Alawites and Shias to capture and behead all those they can get their hands on. ISIL used a fatwa of Ibn Taymiyyah's to justify the public burning alive of Jordanian pilot Muath al-Kasasbeh, for example.

Ibn Taymiyyah, who is called in Saudi and other Salafist schools Sheikh al-Islam, (the grand Sheikh of Islam), is one of the key sources on theological education in Saudi Arabia, and Saudi sponsored religious schools around the world.

—*Hussein Askary*

Schubert's *Schwanengesang* And the Manhattan Project

by Dennis Speed

The silver Swan, who, living, had no Note,
when Death approached, unlocked her silent throat.
Leaning her breast upon the reedy shore,
Thus sang her first and last, and sang no more:
"Farewell, all joys! O Death, come close mine eyes!
More Geese than Swans now live, more Fools than Wise."

—Lyrics to a Madrigal
by Orlando Gibbons (1583-1625)

Nov. 23—It is nearly impossible to produce great art in a society dominated by fools. In a society dominated by such as Barack Obama, reproducing Classical principles of great art, and of music in particular, to reintroduce these principles into the daily experience of Americans, is, though a daunting task, also a moral necessity of the first order.

Capitulation to the deadly banality of today's "popular culture" need not be our society's only choice. The Schiller Institute demonstrated on Saturday evening, November 21, in a Manhattan "music evening," that true creativity, produced by geniuses such as the composer Franz Schubert (who died 187 years ago on November 19 at the age of 31), can be experienced, captured, reproduced, and transmitted by a dedicated ensemble that is selflessly intent on "communicating and receiving intense and impassioned conceptions respecting man and nature" to their fellow citizens.

Schiller Institute

Tenor Everett Suttle, being accompanied by Cheryl Berard at the piano. Seated to the right are John Sigerson (center) and Frank Mathis.

The Song Cycle as a Whole

This presentation of Schubert's collected last songs, *Schwanengesang*, D. 957, was unusual. Three singers, tenors John Sigerson and Everett Suttle, and baritone Frank Mathis, jointly performed the cycle, the which consists primarily of the works of three poets contemporary with Schubert: Ludwig Rellstab, Heinrich Heine, and Jacob Seidl. That interaction, and its evolution over the course of the fourteen songs that comprise the whole, culminated in Suttle's very effective singing of *"Die Taubenpost"* (probably Schubert's last composed song). This made accessible to the 80 people in attendance—a perfect-sized audience for an authentic "Schubertiade"—not merely the songs, or the "song cycle," but also the discovery, through the musicians themselves, including accompanist Cheryl Berard, of the process of discovery of the composition as a whole.

It was remarked upon by the musicians that not only was the audience unusually attentive, following each song very carefully, equipped in many cases with English translations of the text. But beyond mere attention, the audience was engaged in working through the living medium of the minds and the voices of the musicians, to grapple with the devastating musical irony often lurking just behind "the words of the poems," behind their musical settings. This is what William Empson, in his *Seven Types of Ambiguity*, alludes to when he says: *"Metaphor…* is the normal mode of development of a language."

Metaphor, and therefore poetry, rather than symbolism, "imagery," or mere "tuned words," is the only reli-

Schiller Institute

Tenor John Sigerson, being accompanied by Cheryl Berard.

able means for the presentation of truly human ideas,—and metaphor was present in this performance. At the conclusion of the program, one audience member remarked to Everett Suttle that he had decided to watch the concert by concentrating on Suttle's changing facial expressions, as that tenor, with increasing delight, watched his colleagues, Sigerson and Mathis—and implicitly himself—perform the cycle's successive songs, not as "pieces," but as a singularity,—a single unity of effect.

The Power of Beauty

Soprano Michelle Fuchs preceded the *Schwanengesang* with three Schubert *Lieder*: *"Im Frühling," "Frühlingsglaube,"* and *"Du bist die Ruh"* ("Springtime," "Spring Faith," and "You Are Repose"). How a concert, or any other presentation of an important idea begins, is all-important in terms of what follows. There were several beautiful things done here; let one example from *"Frühlingsglaube"* (Spring Faith) suffice.

The poetic line *"Nun muss sich alles, alles wenden"* is changed completely the second time—as the line

Schiller Institute

The Schubert Evening was opened by soprano Michelle Fuchs, accompanied by Margaret Greenspan at the piano.

of poetry itself compels. The listener first hears the poetic idea, and then hears it differently, because Schubert the composer musically does, what the poetical idea "says"—"now must *all things* change." Fuchs and accompanist Margaret Greenspan fully performed this metaphor, without calling any attention to it. This was done even more so in *"Du bist die Ruh"* (You Are Repose). Each of the three opening Schubert songs built upon the meaning of the other, providing the platform for the *Schwanengesang* song-cycle.

Diane Sare, founder and director of the New York Schiller Institute Community Chorus, and member of the Policy Committee of the LaRouche Political Action Committee, pointed out that several musicians, including those involved in this performance, began a collaboration with the Schiller Institute less than a year ago for the purpose of supplanting the non-stop ugliness of fear/hatred presently sweeping the nation and the world. To that end, the project of recruiting hundreds, and even thousands, to what Lyndon LaRouche has termed "the Manhattan Project" by means of their participation in building and becoming members of the Community Chorus, has improved the attention span, and moral depth, of those that have taken up this challenge to the normal death-culture that is promulgated daily as "entertainment."

"Entertainment,"—such as the violent video-games which have become the major pre-requisite for joining a military which is now being rapidly transformed in certain sections into death-squads,—requires an anti-musical, anti-creative mind-set. The American citizens' ability to understand Russia, China, India, and the New Silk Road/World Land-Bridge, will increase dramatically as this process of chorus recruitment is brought to fruition in Manhattan.

While several professional musicians who attended the Schubertiade were very happy about the quality of the performances, conductor Sare emphasized that "the audience was as intense as the performers." The Saturday Manhattan project dialogue with Lyndon La-Rouche, the music classes using the Italian *solfeggio* method, and the organizing of "the 1,500-person chorus," are now mutually reinforcing processes in a singular "field" called Manhattan—and this can become the musical means by which to defeat the submission to "fear itself" that is presently "paralyzing needed efforts to convert retreat into advance" throughout the United States of Obama-who-must-be-removed.

FIDELIO

Journal of Poetry, Science, and Statecraft

From the first issue, dated Winter 1992, featuring Lyndon LaRouche on "The Science of Music: The Solution to Plato's Paradox of 'The One and the Many,' " to the final issue of Spring/Summer 2006, a "Symposium on Edgar Allan Poe and the Spirit of the American Revolution," *Fidelio* magazine gave voice to the Schiller Institute's intention to create a new Golden Renaissance.

The title of the magazine, is taken from Beethoven's great opera, which celebrates the struggle for political freedom over tyranny. *Fidelio* was founded at the time that LaRouche and several of his close associates were unjustly imprisoned, as was the opera's Florestan, whose character was based on the American Revolutionary hero, the French General, Marquis de Lafayette.

Each issue of *Fidelio*, throughout its 14-year lifespan, remained faithful to its initial commitment, and offered original writings by LaRouche and his associates, on matters of, what the poet Percy Byssche Shelley identified as, "profound and impassioned conceptions respecting man and nature."

Back issues are now available for purchase through the Schiller Institute website:
http://www.schillerinstitute.org/about/order_form.html

Every Day Counts In Today's Showdown To Save Civilization